KNEELERS

ALSO BY ELIZABETH BINGHAM

with Mary Morgan
Remarkable Churches near Hay-on-Wye

Kneelers

THE UNSUNG FOLK ART OF ENGLAND AND WALES

Elizabeth Bingham

Chatto & Windus

LONDON

1 3 5 7 9 10 8 6 4 2

Chatto & Windus, an imprint of Vintage, is part of the
Penguin Random House group of companies whose addresses can be found at
global.penguinrandomhouse.com

Penguin
Random House
UK

First published by Chatto & Windus in 2023

penguin.co.uk/vintage

Extracts from 'The Stately Homes of England', *The Operette*, 'Mad Dogs and
Englishmen' and 'Mrs Worthington' by Noël Coward, © Warner/Chappell
Music by permission of Alan Brodie Representation Ltd
www.alanbrodie.com

Extract from 'Hunter Trials' © The Estate of John Betjeman 1995, 1958, 1960,
1962, 1964, 1966, 1968, 1970, 1979, 1981, 1982, 2001

A CIP catalogue record for this book is available from the British Library

HB ISBN 9781784743963

Printed and bound in Latvia by Livonia Print

The authorised representative in the EEA is Penguin Random House Ireland,
Morrison Chambers, 32 Nassau Street, Dublin D02 YH68

Penguin Random House is committed to a sustainable future for our business,
our readers and our planet. This book is made from Forest Stewardship
Council® certified paper.

FSC
www.fsc.org
MIX
Paper from
responsible sources
FSC® C018179

To my family

CONTENTS

Preface

THE MOST WIDELY practised form of folk art in England and Wales over the last ninety years has been the designing and making of church kneelers and cushions.

Begun in the 1930s at Winchester Cathedral with the magnificent seat cushions and kneelers designed by Sybil Blunt, completed to wide publicity in 1938, the practice spread first and slowly to other cathedrals. Then the Second World War meant all decorative stitching gave way to more practical uses. Even those who had never done much sewing managed to make-do and mend, to adapt clothes for growing children and to use ingenuity to make a little go a long way.

The young Queen's coronation in 1953 relaunched enthusiasm for celebrating both past and present in Anglican parishes across England and Wales. Chelsea Old Church, London, is a prominent example, celebrating not only the coronation but its own rebuilding. Its kneelers became famous and helped to spur on the new countrywide enthusiasm for the craft.

Professional designers of ecclesiastical embroidery were eager to lay down rules for how new kneelers were to be designed. Joan Edwards – who twenty years later compiled the best book on kneeler-making yet written – wrote in 1967 an uncharacteristically boring book on how a parish should approach a kneeler project. First, she instructed, the church architect should be asked to advise. If in his [sic] view a proposed design was weak, a new designer should be brought in. Simplicity was the objective. She supplied a number of patterns to be used, all confined to a few straight lines.

Across the country, parishes were cheerfully ignoring the experts and focusing on their local concerns. Wildlife and plants were popular. Local designs featured pubs and shops as well as castles and factories. The slip road to the A14 was clearly important to the parish it served. Bridges were popular together with important local buildings.

The Second World War is vividly recorded with ARP wardens – firefighters during the bombings – joining motifs from all the armed services. In some parishes, up to 10 per cent of the kneelers are linked to the war, and many of the stitchers had fought in it.

Local myths and mythical beasts include sinister dragons whose tails end with the heads of blonde women. A kneeler showing the fabled couple Simon and Nellie quarrelling over a piece of dough records the invention of the Simnel cake.

Aside from plants and wildlife, favourite stories from the Bible were frequently featured. The Garden of Eden, Noah's Ark, Jonah and the Whale and the Three Kings have been regularly depicted. Old Testament accounts of Joseph and his coat of many colours, of David and Goliath, and of Daniel in the lions' den also appear in many churches. The sacred is avoided. Kneelers and seat cushions are concerned with the cheerful: the solemn aspects of Christianity are not felt suitable for sitting on or for being kicked about on the floor.

I first realised that the practice was endangered when, on a visit to Cornwall in the 1980s, I found that church after church – ancient, Victorian, vast, tiny – had identical kneelers with crude designs carried out in big stitches. The specialist shops that once supplied canvaswork materials and advice had been squeezed out of business by high rents, so manufacturers of kneeler kits appeared to many congregations to be the only source of wools and canvas.

Naively I thought that all that was needed was a website to explain how simple it was to design a kneeler, where to source the materials and the fact that the cost was a third cheaper than buying a kit. I thought that saving money would encourage congregations to embark on kneeler-making. To help novice designers, I would add photographs of interesting kneelers that I had come across. And so, some thirty years ago, I set up the Parish Kneelers website, parishkneelers.co.uk, to support the practice of designing and stitching church kneelers that were local, original and unique.

My humble website proved unequal to the task of resisting commercial advertising. People continued to pay more than they needed to for designs far weaker than they could – with pencil, rubber and a sheet of graph paper – have worked up for themselves. The tide of kneelers made using commercial kits swamped more and more churches. Over time, however, as visitors to my website alerted me to the original work being created in their parishes, I realised that there was a need to record a vanishing folk art. And so my gallery of original kneelers grew and grew.

Eventually, I discovered that on Parish Kneelers I had amassed a vivid record of the social history of the second part of the twentieth century. And yet, finally, the twenty-first century is seeing the disappearance of this unique art form. Modernising clerics are removing pews in favour of chairs that can easily be cleared to create space for social activities. Few chairs are designed to accommodate kneelers and chairs themselves fail to make kneeling easy. Kneeling with your nose in someone else's back does not promote spiritual thoughts. And only small contortionists can manage to kneel in the rows of chairs in Westminster Abbey's transepts. Thus kneelers and kneeler-makers are becoming redundant.

The Anglican Church protects its crockets and corbels but only protects ecclesiastical textiles such as altar frontals and embroidered vestments. Canvaswork cushions and kneelers have no ecclesiastical purpose and can be dumped at will by modernising pastors. In Derby Cathedral, the 1,500 canvaswork kneelers for the nave, designed by Jane Page, are now languishing in store. In Winchester, some of Sybil Blunt's magnificent choir-stall cushions are also locked away. In Chelsea Old Church, the kneeler honouring Leighton and Prue Thomson, the organisers – among much else – of the kneeler project, is lost, believed stolen. In Hereford Cathedral, the first kneelers by Mrs Smith were downgraded. In many parish churches, fine folk-art kneelers have been put into storage or binned.

The church of St John the Baptist at Cirencester, Gloucestershire, is an exception. It has recognised that most of its congregation will not wish to kneel but – hooray – was unwilling to dispose of its splendid kneelers. The old-fashioned can still collect a kneeler with their hymn book on the way in.

I would welcome the loss of the kneelers patiently and expensively made from commercial kneeler kits. But I mourn the loss of kneelers made – often to humble and clumsy designs – by stitchers enchanted by local wildlife or activities or landmarks, as of course I sorrow at the loss of folk and community art's finer examples. These are to be welcomed and protected, one hopes, from the indifference of later generations.

Some kneelers, of course, are more than folk art. Sylvia Green produced glorious kneelers in London's St Michael, Highgate, and elsewhere. The Winchester Cathedral choir-stall cushions and kneelers, designed by Sybil Blunt, and the Lancaster Priory choir-stall backs, cushions and kneelers by Guy Barton, are among the highlights of twentieth-century textile art.

Textile art is frequently disparaged by 'proper' artists and art historians: the Royal Academy ruled in 1770 that exhibitions should not include needlework. Sybil Blunt, whose designs for Winchester Cathedral launched the explosion of interest in creating church kneelers, also designed the magnificent Women's Institute Tapestry illustrating the work of women during the Second World War. It is held in store by the Imperial War Museum in London where it is catalogued under 'Souvenirs and Ephemera', either because – like the eighteenth-century Royal Academy – the museum does not recognise textile art as 'Art' or because of unconscious misogyny. At least the Imperial War Museum has put its tapestry on the internet – something that Winchester Cathedral and Lancaster Priory have yet to do.[1]

David Hockney is a rare advocate of textile art. In an email to Martin Gayford, published at the front of *Spring Cannot Be Cancelled: David Hockney in Normandy*, he describes his visits to the Bayeux Tapestry: '[…] a marvellous

St John the Baptist, Cirencester

work without a vanishing point or shadows (when did they begin, is my question to the art historians?). We then went to Angers and saw the Apocalypse Tapestry (also no shadows), and then in Paris we saw the unicorn tapestries. So within a week we had seen three of Europe's greatest tapestries.'[2] He recognises that textiles can be art. Would that others would open their eyes!

The expression 'folk art' conjures up images of macramé hangings and patchwork boleros. But it's hard to find a generic term for the armies of amateur designers who seized pencil, rubber and graph paper to create the country's vast collection of unique church kneelers. The formidable Daphne Nicholson of Hereford Cathedral would probably be insulted by the term but her colleague, Mrs Sawley, who designed the glorious memorial kneelers at St Michael and All Angels, Onibury, Shropshire, might not have objected. Enid Money of Quenington, Gloucestershire, and Elaine Nason of Laxfield, Suffolk, perhaps never thought of themselves as 'folk artists': they were just people who volunteered to get a parish project off the ground. Locals and visitors delight in their designs. The memorial kneeler in Chelsea Old Church for Thomas More's Fool is noted for being stitched by the actor Ernest Thesiger; the reputation of Miss Gow who designed it remains obscure. George Insley, who designed the beautiful cushions at St Clare, Bradfield St Clare, Suffolk, in his retirement, had never previously painted or embroidered.

The partnerships of Sybil Blunt and Louisa Pesel in Winchester, and Guy and Maire Barton in Lancaster Priory, led to outstanding designs and canvaswork, but George Insley's seat cushions and altar-rail kneelers which he stitched for Bradfield St Clare are also superb. Will their canvaswork continue to be protected by admiring congregations? As mentioned some of Sybil Blunt's great choir-stall cushions have been stored away.

This book records the preoccupations of different parishes in different decades and some of the delights of what has been achieved before kneelers are tidied away for good. It is a nostalgic look at a time when the Anglican Church in a fit of absent-mindedness accommodated this vigorous movement of folk art.

'Springtime' by George Insley.
St Clare, Bradfield St Clare

KNEELERS ARE FOR KNEELING ON

Christians through the centuries have had different views on the appropriate stance for addressing the Almighty. In his book *From the Holy Mountain*, William Dalrymple maintains that the early Christians prayed on their knees, prostrating themselves so that their heads touched the ground.[3] This was the practice he came across in the Armenian monastery of Mor Gabriel in Turkey, founded at the end of the fourth century.

Dalrymple had adopted as his guidebook to the eastern Mediterranean a travel memoir and collection of anecdotes by the monk John Moschus, written at a time when Byzantium was under threat from east and west. As Islam gradually replaced Orthodox, Armenian and Syriac Christianity, it adopted their form of worship with prayer mats softening the ground for prostrations.

Had Christians not moved away from this earlier style of praying, the kneeler-makers of the second half of the twentieth century would have been stitching prayer mats rather than the smaller and quicker-to-make kneelers.

Kneelers soften the ground for the knees of worshippers, but early hermits and saints scorned this rejection of hardship. The fourth-century historian Eusebius recorded that the Apostle James spent so long kneeling in prayer that 'his knees became hard like those of a camel'.

Christians who were more protective of their knees turned to hassocks – defined in the Oxford English Dictionary as a 'firm tuft or clump of matted vegetation [...] such as occurs in boggy ground; a "tussock"'. The Dictionary continues: 'hassocks in bogs were formerly taken up [...] shaped, trimmed and dressed [...] to make kneeling much easier than on the pavement of the church. [...] hassocks of turf or peat, formerly used in the church, are [...] preserved at Lower Gravenhurst in Bedfordshire.'[4] And there they are still, two clumps of matted vegetation now displayed in glass cases.

The word 'hassock' began to fall out of favour once Cardinal Newman introduced the new word 'kneeler' in 1848. It certainly no longer refers to matted vegetation.

A hassock made by the author.

My Introduction to Kneeler-making

ALL HALLOWS BY THE TOWER

My inauguration into kneeler-making was in the late 1960s, when I embarked with others on a kneeler project for the church of All Hallows by the Tower in the City of London. The vicar described its parishioners as 'a gathered congregation' since local residents in the City were scarce. This meant that kneeler-makers never came together in cosy weekly groups and most communications – in those pre-internet days – were by post. I didn't know where to start, but Chelsea Old Church was widely famed for its kneelers, so I decided to ask advice from that fount of authority.

Miss Moberly-Bell, the doyenne of the church's needleworkers, invited me to tea. I knew it would be a difficult occasion since I had an energetic one-year-old in tow. My hostess was bound to have a room filled with low tables carrying beautiful and vulnerable ornaments – a young mother's nightmare. I arrived to find my prediction alarmingly accurate, but I had also arrived with a solution. Miss Moberly-Bell tried to engage in introductory conversational formalities, but I was on my hands and knees on the floor strapping my daughter into her baby bouncer. Once I had her clipped onto the door frame, full of apologies, I was able to engage in similar polite talk.

But conversation proved difficult.

'What do you use to stuff the kneelers?' I asked.

'Is she really safe there?' my hostess worried.

'What size of canvas is best?' I ventured.

'Can she get out if she wants to?' Miss Moberly-Bell enquired.

'I've never heard of chip foam,' I volunteered.

'I've never seen a baby bouncer,' Miss Moberly-Bell declared.

Meanwhile my daughter Kate burbled and bounced.

Eventually we agreed on essentials. Yes, Kate was safe and enjoying herself. Yes, canvas of ten squares to the inch and high-density chip foam was a desirable basis for a kneeler project.

In those days, people were happy to count so we all depended on pencilled-in patterns on graph paper. Like Chelsea Old Church, we decided to focus on people with a link to the church as the inspiration for our kneeler designs. All Hallows is the oldest church in the City of London so there was a huge choice of potential subjects. Some may have worshipped here, been buried here or have even been beheaded just outside on Tower Hill, where prominent courtiers who had lost favour with the Tudor Crown were executed. Others had a more significant connection. These are some of my kneelers which, along with many others created at the same time, are still used in the church.

This kneeler, one of my favourites, celebrates Thomas Cruso, a friend of Daniel Defoe. Robinson Crusoe borrowed his name but here he is remembered by Man Friday's alarming footprint.

I enjoyed working out the design for this sixteenth-century Venetian Consul in London who was an occasional attender at All Hallows, but I could not manage the perspective of the ferro – the metal device on the prow.

Francis Chichester (1901–72), the first person to circumnavigate the globe single-handedly, set off in January 1967 in his sailing boat from nearby Tower Hill. He returned to Plymouth by way of Cape Horn in just 226 days.

Henry Howard, Earl of Surrey, KG (1516/17– 47), was a distinguished poet but also an ambitious politician, once described by a historian as 'the most foolish proud boy that is in England'.[5] Henry VIII charged him with treason for adding Edward the Confessor's coat of arms to his own – thus claiming royal inheritance. He and his father were imprisoned in the Tower and sentenced to be executed. Henry Howard was beheaded on 19 January 1547, but his father survived because Henry VIII died before the second execution could be carried out.

Robert Devereux, 2nd Earl of Essex (1565–1601), was much favoured by Queen Elizabeth I but fell dramatically from favour following the humiliating failure of his campaign to restore royal authority in Ireland. He then led an unsuccessful rising in London, leading to his execution for treason in 1601.

Grinling Gibbons (1648–1721), the Michelangelo of wood carving, was paid £12 to carve the magnificent font cover for All Hallows by the Tower.

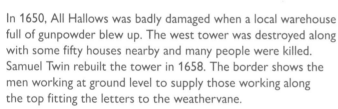

In 1650, All Hallows was badly damaged when a local warehouse full of gunpowder blew up. The west tower was destroyed along with some fifty houses nearby and many people were killed. Samuel Twin rebuilt the tower in 1658. The border shows the men working at ground level to supply those working along the top fitting the letters to the weathervane.

Samuel Pepys (1633–1703), as naval administrator, used the new All Hallows tower to check on the extent of the Great Fire of London of 1666 with its potential threat to the dockyards.

BOUGHROOD

My second kneeler project, a decade or two later, was for the peaceful rural parish of St Cynog, Boughrood, in Radnorshire, Wales. This is where we spent our holidays and the place to which I retired. For this series of kneelers, I attempted to illustrate the Benedicite – the song sung by Shadrach, Meshach and Abednego when Nebuchadnezzar had them cast into the fiery furnace.

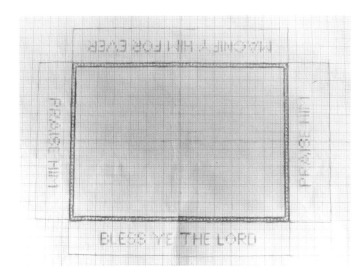

This is our template. The lettering on the sides was constant though colours and patterns changed.

Brechfa Pool, in the shape of a dewdrop to mark 'Dews and Frosts', is a joy for skaters. There is a portrait of the author in the bottom right.

O YE MOUNTAINS & HILLS

'Mountains and Hills' was straightforward for one whose view was bounded by the Black Mountains and the Brecon Beacons.

As a community project it was unsuccessful, since my weekdays in London prevented me from organising the stitching get-togethers at which novice stitchers could get help from those more expert and where everyone could suggest subjects and try out designs. Several patient stitchers helped me out, but before we could complete the final verses it was decided to remove a number of pews. And there was no space for further kneelers.

How to illustrate the Powers of the Lord? I decided that the Creator should be indicated by the border demonstrating the complexity of creation; that the Redeemer should be indicated by the central border of crosses; and that the Comforter should be indicated by the five-light candlesticks in the corner. But OOPS! One of the corners only has a three-light candlestick. Folk artists sometimes get things wrong!

I copied the men and the cows from a Middle Eastern carpet. I particularly like the cows.

Where It All
Began

WADHAM COLLEGE CHAPEL

The history of decorated church kneelers and seat cushions begins in the seventeenth century. The first ones recorded the symbols or coats of arms of benefactors and were made in Turkey work. This is the term given to wool-work in which the yarns are knotted as in carpets to create a pile and are not woven or stitched.

The oldest example appears to be two Turkey-work kneelers made for Wadham College, Oxford. They were made in honour of the college's founders, Nicholas and Dorothy Wadham, and of King James VI and I who gave welcome support to the widowed Dorothy's efforts.

Nicholas and Dorothy Wadham were prosperous Somerset landowners. Nicholas had been educated at Oxford and, as the marriage was childless, the two decided that part of their estate should be devoted to founding a new college there. Nicholas died in 1609 before arrangements had been made but Dorothy declared her intention to proceed with their plan. This was met with bitter hostility from her brother-in-law who felt strongly that the family estates should not be diminished for anything so absurd. In due course the dispute was raised at court, with the Bishop of Bath and Wells lobbying strongly for Dorothy. The King agreed, writing in Dorothy's support to Oxford City Council, the owner of the site that she had chosen. Thus, in 1610, Wadham College was founded, the first Oxford college to be created in the reign of the Stuarts.

Wadham College Chapel was completed in 1613, except for its stained-glass windows. Dorothy Wadham showed her gratitude for the King's support by mounting his statue on the entrance arch of the Inner Court, above the statues of herself and her late husband. At the summit, she displayed the Stuart coat of arms.

When the Hanoverian dynasty replaced the Stuarts, the coat of arms was prudently changed. Possibly at the same time, its two college kneelers with their Stuart associations may also have been transferred to the archives. This would explain their survival in such excellent condition.

This blue kneeler honoured the King, the initials IR at the top of the kneeler standing for Iacobus Rex. The double rose and the lions refer to his Tudor inheritance. The little birds on each side of the rose are an engaging extra.

The second kneeler shows elements from the Wadham family's coat of arms, in particular the white flowers. The border round the central motif would have been black, but at that time black was achieved by steeping the wool in a solution of soot, and soot gradually erodes wool.

BERLIN WORK

In 1643, the Protestant-minded Corporation of Norfolk commissioned 'twenty six cushens' with the arms of the City for the Mayor and Aldermen at their new preaching place, the Dutch Chapel. These were seat cushions and not intended to be used for what they considered to be the Romish practice of kneeling during prayer.

After the Restoration in 1660, Brasenose College, Oxford, and Pembroke College, Cambridge, received armorial cushions from benefactors. Those in Pembroke College were bequeathed by Matthew Wren, Bishop of Ely, who also left '12 Turkey-work cushions' to Jesus College, Cambridge. Its Master wrote indignantly to the Master of Pembroke demanding to know whether Jesus College would receive 'anything or noe besides ye motheaten Cushions'.[6]

Turkey work required skilled artisans. In the early nineteenth century amateurs embraced the new possibilities for decorative needlework provided by Berlin work. It was a form of needlework using wools in cross stitch or tent stitch (which is half a cross stitch) in which the design can be copied from a graph-paper pattern to canvas by counting the stitches.

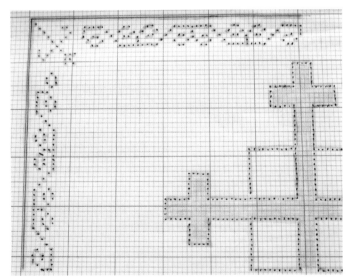

A type of Berlin-work pattern simple to copy by anyone able to count to ten.

The Countess of Wilton, who wrote *The Art of Needlework* in 1840, said that Berlin work was launched in 1804 in Berlin by a print seller with the English-sounding name of Philipson. He was the first to publish coloured graph-paper patterns for canvaswork. While the Napoleonic Wars raged, ladies across Europe and the United States seized on the patterns with unprecedented enthusiasm.

The novelty was not in the designs themselves so much as in the fact that the patterns were coloured. They were printed in black on graph paper, and then women were employed to paint in the colours. The Countess of Wilton remarked on the number of women employed as colorists by the different Berlin-work repositories of the day. The work was far more attractive than many of the jobs – as laundresses, match girls or as 'women kept for rough' – open to women of the period.

The launch of women's magazines – such as the *Englishwoman's Domestic Magazine*, published from 1852 by Mrs Beeton's husband, Samuel Orchart Beeton – helped to popularise patterns for this new craze. New patterns helped to sell magazines, which also advertised new repositories where wools and canvas could be bought and where ladies could spend a social morning browsing the latest designs. The repositories soon found they could promote sales even better by painting the patterns directly onto canvas.

Berlin-work designs grew more elaborate and more flamboyant. New chemical dyes also helped to make them more garish. In 1857, a student named William Perkins had failed in an attempt to make a synthetic version of the anti-malarial drug, quinine, from coal tar. In the process, however, he had produced a powder of an intense mauve which he patented as 'mauveine'. It became so popular that ladies' fashions were said to be infected with 'mauve measles'. Other equally intensely coloured dyes followed. They had an unfortunate effect on Berlin work.

Painted canvas required little or no concentration by the stitcher. If a stitcher was working from a graph-paper pattern, however, it required her close attention. A young lady at her mother's At Home afternoons could not focus on a gentleman visitor while counting – for example – seventeen stitches along, three stitches up, then eight stitches diagonally downwards. How much easier to show off her genteel needlework skills by simply following the pattern painted onto her canvas. The twentieth-century commercial kneeler kits are the successors of this type of Berlin work.

As painted canvases became ever more sentimental and wool colours more garish, there was a reaction among skilled embroiderers. Towards the end of the nineteenth century, 'Art Needlework', inspired by the Pre-Raphaelites and the Arts and Crafts Movement, used a wide variety of stitches to create floral designs based on medieval imagery. Satin stitch on silk materials allowed much greater delicacy of shading and design than was on offer in contemporary Berlin work.

Earlier, whitework and drawn thread work had also become popular, helped by Agnes Blencowe, sister of a Norfolk clergyman. She was visiting a neighbouring church and was startled to see no altar. Where was it? A parishioner

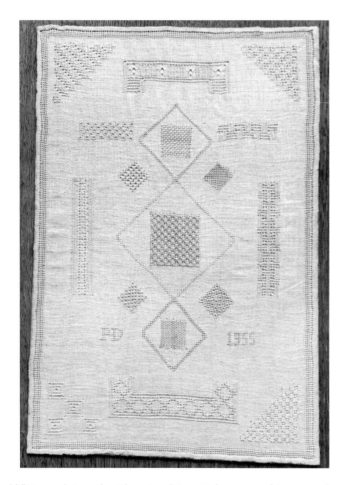

Whitework is embroidery in white stitches on a white ground. Drawn thread work – removing alternate threads from the warp and woof of the sampler – allows further embroidered patterning.

explained that 'their table had been taken out to the cricket match to score on'.

The shocked Miss Blencowe felt that had the altar been properly dressed with the 'fair white linen cloth' required by the Book of Common Prayer, it would not have been treated so casually. She therefore, in 1854, founded the Ladies Ecclesiastical Embroidery Society to 'supply altar cloths of strictly ecclesiastical design either by reproducing ancient examples or by working under the supervision of a competent architect'. Ecclesiastical embroidery was further helped by the foundation in 1872 of the Royal School of Needlework.

Some of the finest vestments were embroidered in 2005 by Derby Cathedral's Embroidery Guild, under the guidance of Canon Leonard Childs. A broken window and a burning cigarette led to a disastrous fire the following year, however, which destroyed all these works along with other historic vestments. Leonard Childs declared his willingness to recreate those he had designed, but he died eleven days later. The altar-rail kneelers he designed, like the one shown opposite, escaped the fire and have survived.

Supporters of the Anglican high church Oxford Movement provided a ready market for embroidered altar frontals and clerical vestments. Elite needleworkers rejoiced in embroidery's new complexity and delicacy, and dismissed Berlin work as old-fashioned – which indeed it was. But it remained hugely popular across a wide segment of society and its practitioners continued to demand painted canvas and brightly coloured wools.

Appletons Wools, founded in the mid-nineteenth century and using both vegetable and aniline dyes, was William Morris' chosen supplier. It also supplied embroidery shops across the country. Readers of Trollope's *The Small House at Allington* will recall that Barchester was unfortunately without such a shop, so that when Lady Rosina de Courcy needed more wool of the right colour she had to rely on her young friend from London, Johnny Eames.[7]

Derby Cathedral altar rail.

REXINE

Kneelers were dramatically altered by the invention of Rexine, an artificial leather, in 1915. Huge numbers of churches welcomed the opportunity to replace straw-stuffed – and mouse-infested – kneelers with ones made from this new hard-wearing fabric.

What parochial church councils did not realise was that the ingredients of the fabric included cellulose nitrate – a low explosive – and alcohol. Rexine, once ignited, burns unstoppably with an intense heat, as happened on 14 July 1951 on an express train near Huntingdon whose seats were upholstered in Rexine, when four carriages were burnt out and twenty-one people injured.

Rexine was also regularly used to make the pads on the paws of teddy bears. Bears and churches have been luckier than the train passengers.

A bear with its distinctive pads.
St Barbara, Earlsdon

Rexine kneeler.

A New Art Form

The first use of canvaswork to decorate cushions and kneelers was for the chapel in the Bishop's Palace in Winchester, Hampshire. It was the inspiration of Theodore Woods, Bishop of Winchester, who in 1931 invited Louisa Pesel to create designs and oversee stitchers to carry them out.

These were so admired that they triggered an invitation from the Dean to produce cushions and kneelers for the cathedral's choir stalls. Louisa Pesel brought in her friend Sybil Blunt to help on the project. But although she had introduced her as 'a very able assistant', Louisa Pesel recognised that Sybil Blunt was outstandingly the better designer and handed over responsibility for designing the choir-stall cushions to her. Louisa Pesel herself took on the role of instructor, training the stitchers who delivered the choir-stall cushions and kneelers.

Sybil Blunt focused on Winchester's history, beginning with the King Arthur of legend. His notional Round Table, actually a thirteenth-century reproduction, hangs in the Great Hall – the only surviving room from Winchester Castle. Many other congregations, inspired by Sybil Blunt, chose to record highlights from their own histories.

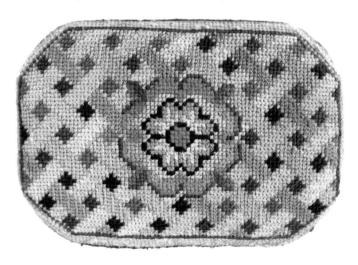

Above and opposite are three examples of Louisa Pesel's many designs for the Bishop's Palace.

The complex background of flowers and geometrical designs is common to all the choir-stall cushions. Note the subtle shifts in the background colour of the cushion opposite. As a single-colour background has a deadening effect, most stitchers mix different shades of wool in their needles, thus enlivening the background through a slight variation.

The medallion records the moment when the dying Arthur has flung Excalibur into the lake but just before the Lady of the Lake has reacted. Alfred, Lord Tennyson, in his poem 'Morte d'Arthur', described:

> *But ere he dipt the surface, rose an arm*
> *Clothed in white samite, mystic, wonderful,*
> *And caught him by the hilt, and brandish'd him*
> *Three times, and drew him under in the mere.* (143–6)

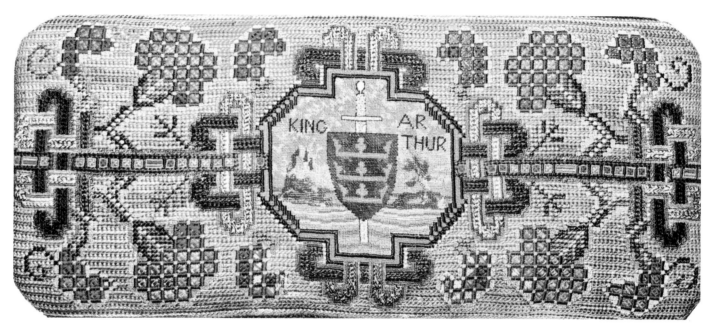

The initial design alters once it meets the golden background. Colours and details are adjusted to meet the requirements of the whole. Louisa Pesel may have supervised the stitchers, but Sybil Blunt clearly supervised the final rendition of the design.

41

A striking cushion is the one that celebrates the contribution of shipping to the local Hampshire economy. Kneeler projects in innumerable parishes took up the theme of local trades and occupations.

The great liner cuts its way through the scattering of tugs, whose smoke obscures the dockyard cranes and the light aircraft overhead. The scarlet of the funnels is picked up by the scarlet of the ship's bottom. The prow is so striking that the eye scarcely takes in the elaborate frame and the cushion's patterned background. The composition of the design did not change between sketch and stitching, but the tugs and grey haze became browner, the cranes on the right became clearer and the blue sky became murkier.

Agriculture was even more important than shipping to Hampshire's economy. Here Sybil Blunt shows not just arable and pastoral emblems but also the essential industrial aspect of the rural economy with its central windmill. The windmill belongs to a Benedictine monastery that draws its wealth from the husbandry of many local manors. Strip farming on the hill on the right of the picture provides grain to be milled and hay to be stacked. The sheep provide wool and manure for the strips. The Winchester economy is thriving.

On the kneeler, Sybil Blunt removed the HUSBANDMEN lettering in the sketch to give a greater sweep of sky.

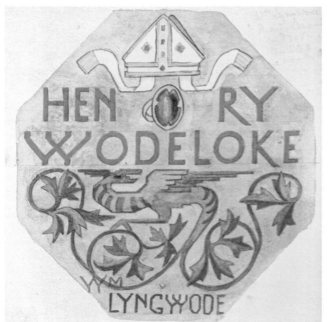

Henry Woodlock (or Wodeloke) was Bishop of Winchester from 1305 until his death in 1316. His episcopal sapphire ring – now in the cathedral museum – is said to be the finest of its kind in Europe. The leafy-tailed dragon can be found rioting among its fellow creatures in the choir stalls. They were carved by William Lyngwode.

The Knights of the Round Table provided Winchester with its first military base. Since then the Royal Hampshire Regiment, the King's Royal Rifle Corps and the Rifle Brigade have been quartered here. Winchester and the cathedral contain many memorials to them. After the Second World War many parishes recorded similar military, naval and air force emblems in memorials to the fallen. The tiger and the rose shown on the left-hand roundel represent the Royal Hampshire Regiment.

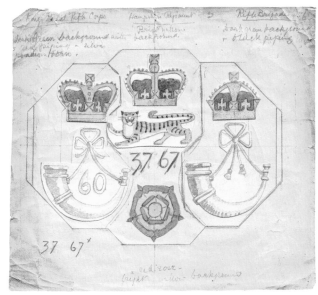

The sketch for the military medallion shows how Sybil Blunt worked out the composition. Since it is a grouping of emblems, the backgrounds could be left to the stitchers to provide the necessary modest colour shifts.

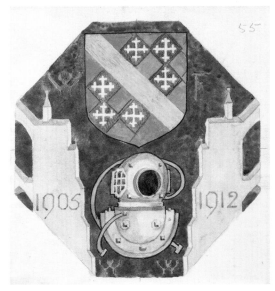

This roundel portrays the diver William Walker, who between 1905 and 1912 shored up the cathedral's foundations. The cathedral was built on peaty soil, and at the beginning of the twentieth century dangerous cracks appeared as the water table began to rise. William Walker worked in full diver's outfit for six hours a day for over six years, moving a total of 900,000 bricks, 114,900 concrete blocks and 25,800 bags of cement. The pillars he built saved the cathedral. The initials and coat of arms belong to Dean William Furneaux, who commissioned the project.

During the Second World War, Louisa Pesel designed kneeler pads now in the cathedral's Epiphany Chapel. The pattern was based on the thirteenth-century tiles in the Retrochoir and the pads were stitched by the girls of Atherley School who had been evacuated from Southampton to Winchester.

Miss Pesel also decided that the pads needed extra stiffening, so instructed the girls to embroider a broad band of cross stitch – to their own designs – that could be attached to the base.

After the war, Louisa Pesel attempted to influence new folk artists by urging stitchers to follow patterns copied

The backgrounds are stitched in varying shades of red. To achieve this, most stitchers use three fine strands of wool in their needle: two dark and one pale; then two pale and one dark. Louisa Pesel was different. She instructed the girls to change the shade in their needles every twenty stitches. For the stitcher, this is profoundly irritating. But schoolgirls were expected to do what they were told, and Miss Pesel was a formidable woman.

In none of the designs for the kneeler base does the background change colour every twenty stitches. And I've never found kneeler pads elsewhere that were embroidered underneath.

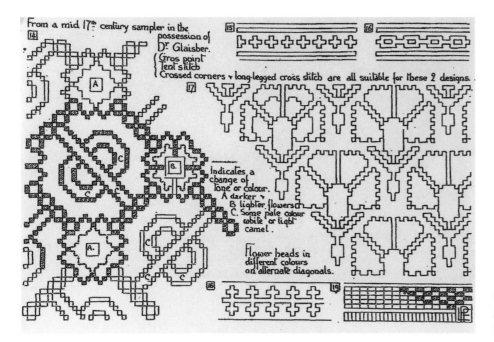

Within the illustration:

From a mid 17th century sampler in the
possession of Dr Glaisher.
(Gros point
Tent stitch
Crossed corners & long-legged cross stitch are all suitable for these 2 designs.

Indicates a
change of
tone or colour.
A darker &
B lighter flowers
C. Some pale colour
white or light
camel.

Flower heads in
different colours
on alternate diagonals.

Illustration from *Historical Designs for Embroidery*, put together from Louisa Pesel's notebooks.

from historic English samplers. She published handbooks of instructions, and encouraged the use of all-over repetitive patterns. She was a traditionalist, not an innovator.

Sybil Blunt, on the other hand, was an artist with an entirely new approach to design. She used the choir stalls as an easel for the display of Winchester's history, from King Arthur to modern times. Her magnificent long seat cushions with pictorial medallions set in elaborate geometric and floral frameworks were completed in 1938, and their influence changed the appearance of innumerable churches across the nation.

The cathedral library houses the Broderers' Scroll – a four-metre illuminated record of the names of over eight hundred people who were involved. At the head of the scroll is that of Louisa Frances Pesel, Mistress of the Embroideries. She had organised the stitchers and probably – with Sybil Blunt – decided on the textural stitches to be used. Second on the scroll comes the name of the Designer, Sybil Allan Blunt. The implication is that the designer is less important than the organiser; it is as if great credit were heaped upon the foreman of the building works at St Paul's Cathedral with Christopher Wren acknowledged merely as the designer.

Landmarks in the Spread of Folk Art

THROUGH THE CHALLENGING war years, Hitler delayed the development of the new form of ecclesiastical embroidery as stitchers on the Home Front were preoccupied with making-do and mending. As post-war austerity eased, however, kneeler-making could resume and stitchers turned to decorative needlework with zeal. Enthusiasm spread from Winchester in the south, to London's Chelsea Old Church in the east, across to Hereford Cathedral in the west, and north to Lancaster Priory, including parishes within and beyond these landmarks.

The coronation of the young Queen in June 1953 marked the beginning of an exuberant movement to beautify churches as hundreds of parishes in England and Wales replaced Rexine and older kneelers with locally designed ones in canvaswork. Thus the second half of the twentieth century saw the flowering of folk art in all its quirkiness and diversity, benignly tolerated by the Anglican Church. Formerly confined to love spoons and corn dollies, it found a new dimension in canvaswork kneelers designed to be local, original and unique. Sybil Blunt's designs for the choir-stall cushions in Winchester were the inspiration.

As folk artists were beavering away across the country, embroidery specialists began to take an interest in church kneelers. Joan Edwards, a lecturer on embroidery at the V&A, published *Church Kneelers* in 1967, containing a variety of designs based on the cross so that stitchers only had to cope with straight lines. She apparently assumed that they would be incapable of dealing with curves or diagonals. I have not yet come across any kneelers that used her patterns.

Joan Edwards continued, however, to take an interest in church kneelers, finding that folk art was springing up all over the country – sometimes good, sometimes clumsy, but always the product of local enthusiasms. She wrote to the *Church Times* in 1984 asking for information on what parishes were producing, and received nearly two hundred replies. From these she was able to compile *A Picture Book for Kneeler Makers* with illustrations, advice and anecdotes from parishes. She included this homily: 'Experienced embroiderers all agree that the bogeyman in kneeler making are [*sic*] the manufacturers and retailers of kits of inferior quality and design, and warn us against using them.' Her *Church Kneeler* book had not sold well. However, her sequel, *A Picture Book for Kneeler Makers*, became the standard work of reference. This book humbly follows in its footsteps.

CHELSEA OLD CHURCH

Chelsea Old Church was one of the first churches after the Second World War to launch a kneeler project. It had been catastrophically bombed during the Blitz in April 1941, with its magnificent collection of wall monuments buried in the debris.

The diocese assumed that there would be no point in trying to rebuild a church that had been so comprehensively destroyed. The Reverend Leighton Thomson, appointed in 1950, disagreed.

All that was left of Chelsea Old Church after the direct hit by a heavy bomb in April 1941.

The five firewatchers killed on 16 April 1941 in the bombing of Chelsea Old Church included a young Canadian, Yvonne Green.

The wall monuments were disinterred and restored. Building materials were somehow amassed and a new church built on the site to the design of the old. With his wife, Prue, he also launched a major project of kneeler-making, with each kneeler honouring someone connected with the church.

The result is a church in which the floor below the pews glows with colour, and historical references abound in a glorious jumble. Notable kneelers include victims of Henry VIII – Sir Thomas More, his son-in-law Giles Heron, his fellow cardinal John Fisher, his printer John Rastell, and his parish priest John Larke, amongst others. More's large family are also all recorded.

The rebuilt church was reopened in May 1958 in a service led by the Bishop of London with the Queen Mother in attendance.

This kneeler would have demanded much patient concentration from both designer and stitcher.

The three kneelers above mark the execution of Sir Thomas More on 6 July 1535; his lute and the rosemary blooming in his garden; 'Tille valle, tilly valle' was the expostulation – taken from the contemporary popular song – used by Thomas More's baffled wife at finding her husband resolute on remaining in the Tower. On the kneeler on the left Sir Thomas More's fool, Henry Patenson, 'a man of special wit, unlike the common sort', appears. He was stitched by the actor Ernest Thesiger.

HEREFORD CATHEDRAL

The first canvaswork kneelers here were designed by Mrs Smith in 1963 for the south transept. She worked out a basic design and elaborated it with textural stitches. But Mrs Smith failed to impress the cathedral authorities. The following year, the Dean launched a campaign to create a Guild of Cathedral Broderers and much time was spent by the Friends of the Cathedral in trying to find a person willing to take it on. Mrs Smith's name was never mentioned.

Poor Mrs Smith! Various people were suggested to lead this and, eventually, Daphne Nicholson took charge. In her monograph on the embroideries in Hereford Cathedral, she said merely that Mrs Smith's kneelers 'are now used elsewhere in the cathedral'. With the help of the vergers, I found them in the Lady Chapel. Mrs Smith may not have been particularly skilled as a designer, but many folk artists are not. She does, however, deserve to be recognised as the first to design and stitch kneelers for the cathedral.

Daphne Nicholson combined Sybil Blunt's talents as a designer with the forceful drive of Louisa Pesel as an organiser. The chancel seat cushions – worked in a variety of stitches – have borders designed after carvings elsewhere in the cathedral. The stall cushions for the cathedral dignitaries reflect their offices.

A basic kneeler designed by Mrs Smith, now relegated to Hereford Cathedral's Lady Chapel.

The Precentor's cushion shows the musical instruments mentioned in Psalm 150.

This kneeler shows the badge of Richard II who gave the Vicars Choral College its Charter.

The front rows of the choir stalls are for the child choristers. Daphne Nicholson said she designed these to be cheerful and fun. They show the birds, animals, insects, frogs and snakes to be found locally.

LANCASTER PRIORY

Some of the finest ecclesiastical canvaswork in the country can be seen in the choir at the medieval Lancaster Priory, formerly the Priory Church of St Mary, at the summit of Castle Hill above the city of Lancaster. The embroideries for the stall backs and panels were designed by Guy Barton with stitching designed by his wife, Maire, who supervised the embroidery group tasked with carrying out her husband's grand vision. The monumental works, which are set in equally magnificent carved oak choir stalls from the fourteenth century, were completed between 1962 and 1977.

The great stall backs focus on the sacred. Through them, the Gospel blazes down, telling the story from the Annunciation to the Resurrection. Since the Virgin Mary is the patron saint of the priory church, all ten of the Gospel stall backs carry a reference to her life.

The Archangel Gabriel kneels to Mary, announcing that she will bear a child who will be the Son of God. The roses lying at Gabriel's feet link Mary with the red rose of Lancaster.

The picture of the Virgin enthroned with the Christ Child is based on the seal of Lancaster Priory, believed to date from the late fourteenth century. The figure below is that of a Benedictine monk.

Mary finds the twelve-year-old Jesus in the Temple. His animated figure contrasts with the rigid figures of the doctors who will be unlikely to agree with the older Christ that love is the fulfilling of the law.

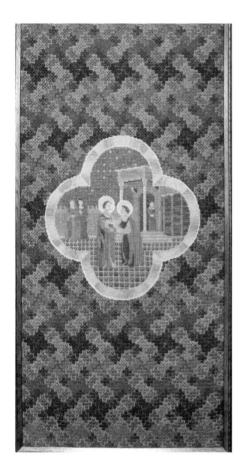

Following the Annunciation, Mary visits her cousin Elizabeth. As Mary greets her, Elizabeth's baby, who will one day become John the Baptist, recognises his future Lord and leaps in the womb for the first time.

Here the risen Christ is shown with the Virgin and an exultant St John. At the base is the chalice surrounded by ears of wheat and the vine of eternal life. The background shows roses, traditionally associated with Mary.

The three Marys visit the tomb on Easter morning, bringing sweet spices to anoint Jesus' body. They are watched over by a Seraph, described in Isaiah as having six wings.

In contrast to the stall backs, the seat backs, cushions and kneelers in Lancaster Priory are not part of the sacred realm. Like misericords, they are only there to provide physical comfort for the congregants. *They are of the earth, earthy* (Cor. 15: 47). Gossipy and quirky, these plebeian cushions and kneelers focus on local interests.

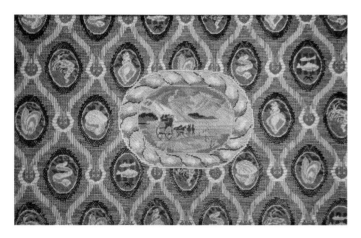

The fishy life in nearby Morecambe Bay features here, together with a bold horse and carriage venturing onto the sands, based on a watercolour by J. M. W. Turner.

The horse and cart, hens and farm animals reflect the importance of the agricultural economy.

Successful Lancaster traders, like Robert Gillow and James Williamson, relied on innovation.

As a young ship's carpenter, Robert Gillow sailed to the Caribbean, discovering the merits and availability of mahogany. On his return, he set himself up as a furniture maker, registering Gillow of Lancaster in 1730. He may have been the first to import mahogany into this country. To make the new wood acceptable to fashionable buyers, it was originally called 'Red Walnut'. The ten chairs are some of Gillow's designs.

James Williamson (1842–1930) was a businessman with many irons in the fire, dealing with batteries and drink and other commodities featured on the cushion. In 1887 he established one of the largest factories in Europe specialising in linoleum. The central coat of arms suggests he had a licence to supply the Prince of Wales.

The central image is of the White Cross works of Storey Brothers Ltd, founded in 1849, of which Heron Chemicals and Colours was a subsidiary. Lancaster Synthetic Silk, marketed as Lansil, was another subsidiary. Decorus made respectable garments. William Goodacre and Sons Ltd, among other businesses, were early twentieth-century manufacturers of coconut matting.

The central emblem shows Lancaster docks. Top left is the ship *Thetis*, a privateer in the Caribbean during the early years of the Napoleonic Wars.[8] She was then converted to a slave ship, making two trips in 1806 and 1807.[9] Bottom left shows a fast clipper. Top right is the first iron-clad ship, the *Wennington*, to be built in Lancaster – like both ships on the left, it relies on sails. Bottom right is a paddle steamer cautiously still keeping its masts.

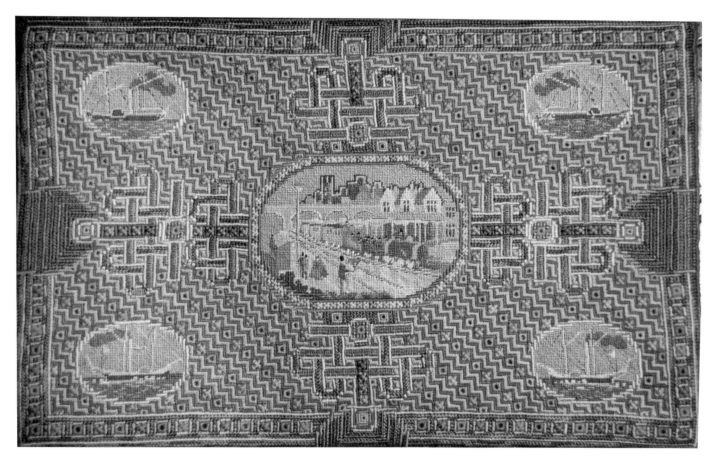

The evolution of steam power is recorded on this cushion. The central image is of the opening of the Lancaster and Carlisle Railway in 1846. In the four corners are steamships, all prudently retaining masts and rigging against emergencies.

The Explosion of
Folk Art

A RANGE OF INTERESTS

Stitchers from all over the country seized on Sybil Blunt's example of creating kneelers that were of immediate relevance to their parish, and following her example, most were pictorial. Usually designs focused on the natural environment but they also recorded local activities and landmarks illustrating the social and technological history of the second half of the twentieth century.

Buildings and Bible stories . . .

St Edmund, Southwold

St Andrew, Much Hadham

Plants and People ...

St Michael and All Angels, Onibury

St Mary Magdalene, Woodstock

Treasurers and Trout ...

Hereford Cathedral

St Margaret, St Margaret's, Herefordshire

AN IMPERFECT WILDLIFE ALPHABET

Stitchers liked recording physical and metaphysical matters, but in parish after parish, what they most preferred was recording their local wildlife.

A is for APPLES
St Michael and All Angels, Onibury

E is for EAGLE
St Michael, Highgate

B is for BEEHIVES
St Mary, Stratford St Mary

C is for COLTSFOOT
St Mary the Virgin, Steeple Barton

D is for DOVE
All Saints, Brandeston

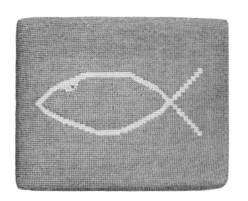

F is for FISH
St Edmund, Acle

G is for GULL
St Andrew, Eaton

H is for HEDGEHOG
St Swithin, Quenington

I is for IRIS
St Cyriac, Lacock

J is for JACOB'S SHEEP
St Peter, Tewin

K is for KINGFISHER
St Mary, Stratford St Mary

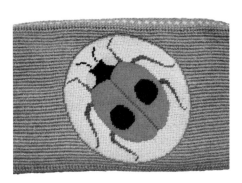

L is for LADYBIRD
St Mary Magdalene, Woodstock

M is for MIAREN MAIR
St David, Llanfaes

N is for NUT
Hereford Cathedral

O is for OWL
St Mary the Virgin, Friston

P is for PIG
St Andrew, Wissett

Q is for QUERCUS
St Peter, Tewin

R is for ROACH
St Mary, Stratford St Mary

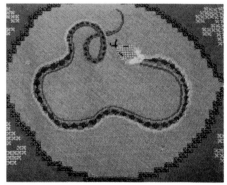

S is for SNAKE
Hereford Cathedral

T is for TITS
St Mary Magdalene, Woodstock

U is for UNICORN
St Michael, Highgate

V is for VIXEN
St Mary Magdalene, Woodstock

W is for WHIPPET
St Peter and St Paul, Deddington

X
All Saints, Brandeston

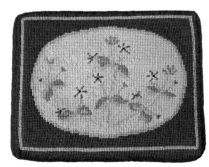

Y is for YELLOW PIMPERNEL
St David, Llanfaes

Z is for ZOO
St Nicholas, Charlwood

Pedants will complain that eagles and unicorns are not commonly to be seen in Highgate and that X and Zoo are not part of any parish's wildlife. Monoglot English readers may object to Briar Rose being named in Welsh but it was stitched by a Welsh stitcher for a Welsh church. Be grateful that the bilingual stitcher also named Gwlyddn Mair Melyn as Yellow Pimpernel. But it is, after all, an imperfect alphabet. Remember the closing words of *Some Like it Hot*: 'Nobody's perfect!'

GENESIS

As well as recording their local environments, congregations wanted to illustrate stories from the Bible.

At St Mary Magdalene, Woodstock, Oxfordshire, they stitched the story of the Creation.

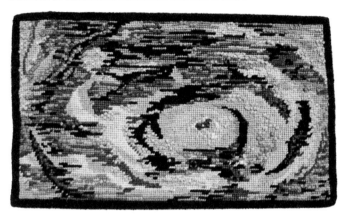

The earth was without form, and void.

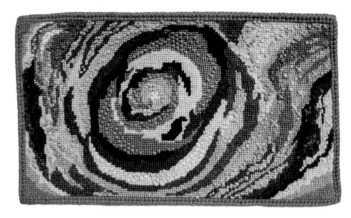

God said: Let there be light.

Let the dry land appear.

Let there be light in the firmament.

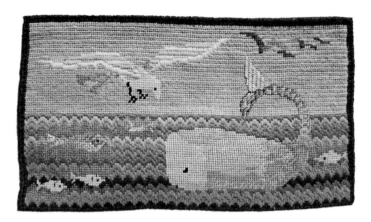

Let the waters bring forth abundantly.

Let us make man in our image. And God saw everything that He had made, and, behold, it was very good. (Gen. 1: 1–31) BUT . . .

The serpent was more subtil than any beast of the field. (Gen. 3: 1).
St Edmund, Acle

 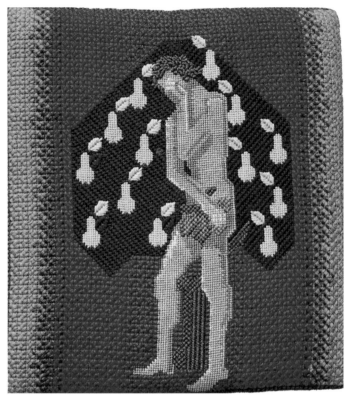

Of Man's First Disobedience, and the Fruit
Of that Forbidden Tree, whose mortal taste
Brought Death into the World, and all our woe…

  Paradise Lost, John Milton, Book 1 (1–3)

St Michael, Highgate

The Serpent wrapped round the Tree of Knowledge

NOAH'S ARK

These are the altar-rail kneelers for the St Nicholas Chapel in Lancaster Priory. Guy and Maire Barton, designers of the superb canvaswork in the chancel, were not involved, but the stitchers that Maire Barton had trained, led by Dorothy Widness, revelled in the opportunity to use their own imaginations.

The Flood followed the Fall. Noah is collecting the animals as the flood waters rise. The birds, whales and dolphins pose no problems but the elephants and reindeer may have to be accommodated in the lower decks; the upper-deck cabins have all been commandeered, the giraffes of course requiring a two-storey cabin. The little green snakes have only just made it to the ladders in time but the poor old tortoises haven't yet reached the gangplank. The osprey is carrying his own food supplies.

Here Noah and Mrs Noah welcome their passengers. The rains are approaching so Mrs Noah hurries to take in the washing, watched by the crocodile who was so anxious to bag a deck-level cabin that she hurried on ahead of her slower-moving partner.

Birds can nest on the deck so the stork and flamingo families can bring all their babies.

All Saints, Laxfield

The rains came and the waters covered the mountains and every living substance was destroyed. But after a hundred and fifty days, *God made a wind to pass over the earth and the waters asswaged* (Gen. 8: 1). Noah waited a further three months stuck on Mount Ararat, then sent out a raven and a dove. The raven never returned and the dove came back exhausted. But after another seven days, the dove – sent out again – returned with an olive leaf. The cautious Noah waited for another seven days then sent the dove out for a third time. She did not return. The waters had dried up. The inhabitants of the ark were released and told to go forth to increase and multiply.

One hopes that Noah warned the snakes to avoid Ireland. He himself lived for a further three hundred and fifty years.

JONAH AND THE WHALE

Even the Flood failed to teach people the error of their ways. God therefore instructed Jonah to go to Nineveh to upbraid the inhabitants for their sins. He refused, hoping to escape God by taking a boat to Tarshish. But once out of reach of land, a great storm made it clear that God was not to be put off.

The stitching on this seat back in Lancaster Priory is as outstanding as the design. Look at the face of Jehovah: eyes, nose and beard indicated and shaped just by the direction of the stitches. A slight tilt of the head is suggested by the arrangement of stitches and by the size of the eyes – the left eye of three stitches and the right of only two. The violent, diagonal shafts of rain are slashed by horizontal squalls, with the stitches reinforcing the colour message.

The sails and spars have been ripped off the ship and scattered across and beyond the border. The tops of the masts are shivered to matchwood. Great billows rear up to port and starboard. Terrified sailors pray and panic. They have failed to notice that the ship is on still waters and the small whale lolls on a calm surface.

But Jonah cannot escape the message. He is targeted by a force field from the hand of God. A mini waterspout makes sure that his attention is engaged. Meanwhile, consider the ship. The smashed masts have been broken at a point where the captain will have no difficulty in jury-rigging a sail. The glass in the cabin windows has not been cracked. No water has landed on the deck. The ship will surely make it to Tarshish. The living tree in Jehovah's hand is the promise of recovery.

Jonah admitted to the captain that he was the cause of the storm and volunteered to be thrown overboard. The crew were happy to oblige.
St Andrew, Much Hadham

Instantly swallowed by a great whale, Jonah spent three days knowing that God's Dial-a-Ride . . .
St Edmund, Acle

. . . was taking him inexorably to NINEVEH.
All Saints, Laxfield

WE THREE KINGS

A mysterious star summons kings from the east to witness the birth of Christ.

The three kings are on their way to Bethlehem. They have been waiting by the palm tree camel stop hoping that – like buses – Bactrian camels come in threes. One king has already got a ride but the other two are still waiting. The kings are – very properly – wearing their crowns but have changed their robes for trousers to make riding easier. The star ensures that they will have no problem finding their way. *St Mary, Stratford St Mary*

Shadows are unusual on kneelers but the star is of course very bright. *All Saints, Laxfield*

Others have failed to get a ride so are having to hurry. *St Giles, Chalfont St Giles*

Some kings prefer horses. *St Mary's, Raydon*

JOY TO THE WORLD

The world rejoices at the beginning of the first millennium.

St Edmund, Southwold

Joseph did whistle and Mary did sing …
And all the bells on earth did ring
For joy our Lord was born.

'As I Sat Under a Sycamore Tree' (trad.)

St Andrew, Much Hadham

St Peter, Langford Budville

St John the Baptist, Metfield

WAR AND EMPIRE

The Old Testament is full of war with Israel resisting or succumbing to foreign occupations. How little the world has changed!

David the shepherd boy takes on Goliath to defeat the Philistines. The latter has failed to consider the ballistic threat. *All Saints, Laxfield*

The New Testament records the time when Palestine was a Roman colony. Victorian-era India was also a colony where British regiments were stationed.

Here the stitcher recalls the presence of the Leicestershire Regiment in India in the nineteenth century.
St Denys, Evington

Indian regiments proved willing to support Britain's war against its European foes. The men of the Baluch Regiment – India's oldest and most decorated regiment – were honoured on English kneelers. *St Peter, Langford Budville*

Many parishes wanted to create a record of the war years. Those on the Home Front wanted to depict the destruction brought about by war. Those who had served in the armed services, however, recoiled from depicting war in all its horror. They preferred to honour fallen comrades through the service emblem that united them.

And when they ask us, and they're certainly going to ask us,
The reason why we didn't win the Croix de Guerre,
Oh! We'll never tell them. No! We'll never tell them
There was a front, but damned if we knew where.

Anonymous (Parody of 'They Didn't Believe Me' by Jerome Kern and Herbert Reynolds)

St Mary Magdalene, Woodstock

St Denys, Evington

St Michael, Framlingham

St Andrew, Wissett

All Saints, Brandeston

St Mary Magdalene, Woodstock

The Consequences of War

Those who fought were eager to show their gratitude for those who supported them in unendurable times.

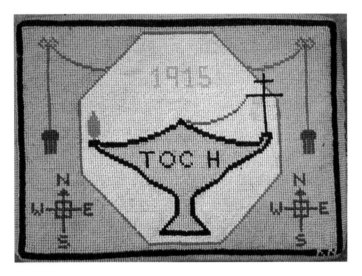

All Hallows by the Tower, London

'Toc H' was signaller's code for Talbot House, a soldiers' rest and recreation centre founded by the Reverend Philip Thomas Byard Clayton CH MC FSA, known as Tubby, and the Reverend Neville Talbot in December 1915. The large house in Poperinge was a few miles behind the front line at Ypres, Belgium.

'All rank abandon, ye who enter here' was inscribed above the door of the chaplains' room. For many exhausted soldiers it was a desperately needed oasis of peace and support after the horror of the trenches. An Upper Room chapel offered spiritual comfort.

After the war, Toc H became a Christian fellowship dedicated to the 'four points of the Christian compass:

Friendship – 'To love widely'
Service – 'To build bravely'
Fairmindedness – 'To think fairly'
The Kingdom of God – 'To witness humbly'

Tubby Clayton died on 16 December 1972. I took a neighbour, a member of Toc H, to his funeral at All Hallows by the Tower, where Tubby had been vicar. The mood at the service was triumphant – Tubby had crossed the river of Jordan and we could almost hear the trumpets welcoming him on the other side.

This cushion honours the plastic surgeon Archibald Hector McIndoe CBE FRCS, whose skill transformed the lives of many from the UK and from Allied countries who were crippled by catastrophic burns.

McIndoe was a plastic surgeon from New Zealand attached to the RAF during the Second World War and based at the Queen Victoria hospital in East Grinstead, Sussex. Airmen in crashed aircraft often suffered from very deep burns and serious facial disfigurement like loss of eyelids. Horrific injuries often caused equally serious psychological suffering.

McIndoe's innovative treatments and skilled surgery gave new life to his patients. In his honour they founded the Guinea Pig Club – a drinking club with membership open to:

St Clement Danes, City of London

The Guinea Pigs – any member of Allied Aircrew who had undergone at least two operations at the Queen Victoria hospital for burns or other crash injuries.

The Scientists – doctors, surgeons and members of medical staff.

The Royal Society for the Prevention of Cruelty to Guinea Pigs – friends and benefactors who made the life of a Guinea Pig a happy one.

Lest We Forget

Following the First World War, tens of thousands of war memorials were erected across the country with the roll of death updated following the Second World War. Many were recorded on church kneelers. Members of the armed forces may have died anywhere across the widespread theatres of war, but in death they were reunited with their old neighbours in the place where they had lived.

One of the tragedies that the two World Wars imposed on Germany is that there are no similar memorials in that country. Families and communities have nowhere to centre their grief. It is as if the dead had to be forgotten.

St Peter, Tewin

St Mary, Stratford St Mary

St Mary Magdalene, Woodstock

St Bartholomew, Chipping

The Royal Air Force church in the City of London – St Clement Danes – has rows of kneelers marked just with the initials of each of those who died. They were stitched by someone who had loved the person remembered. Each stitcher could invent their own design.

John Grayburn's mother commemorates her son.
Chalfont St Giles, St Giles

The Burma Star was awarded to those who had fought the Japanese in the Burmese jungles. Many recipients had been prisoners of war in brutal conditions. Some of the survivors struggled with psychological wounds as damaging as physical ones. *St Constantine, Constantine*

PEACETIME

The world changed. Slowly the country rebuilt itself after the long years of privation. Access to education expanded and the new National Health Service made glasses – as well as its other resources – available to all.

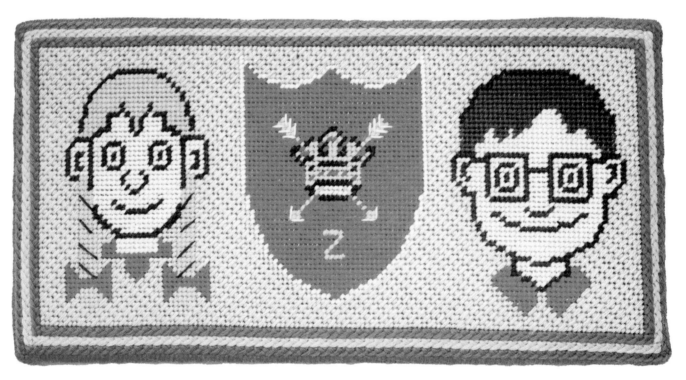

St Edmund, Southwold

But change could be confusing and dramatic, and sometimes brought loss. Before the Second World War, almost every village had a shop – where else could you get your tea and order your Cash's name tapes? After the war, supermarkets expanded and many village shops disappeared.

Before the war, builders and farmers were dependent on the village blacksmith for making and repairing their tools and for shoeing their horses. As tractors replaced horses, most blacksmiths redeveloped their forges as garages, selling and repairing the new means of transport.

St Andrew, Much Hadham

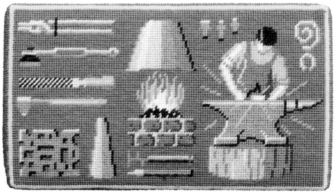

St Peter, Langford Budville

Post-war homes depended on open fires for warmth. Later, new sources of energy were developed.

Sizewell nuclear power station near Southwold in Suffolk.
St Edmund, Southwold

Armchairs in front of an open fire.
St Andrew, Congham

A North Sea oil rig near Wissett in Suffolk.
St Andrew, Wissett

FARMING: CHANGE AND CONTINUITY

Before the war, farming depended to a large extent on muscle power. Horses provided most of this power, but until the arrival of tractors, farmers had to pitch hay onto carts and cut hedges with hooks. It was usually their womenfolk who milked the cows.

Horsepower gave way to mechanised power and farming was transformed. Tractors replaced muscle power.

St Andrew, Much Hadham

St Mary the Virgin, Steeple Barton

Milking was no longer carried out by hand. The new electric milking parlours meant that churns were replaced by milk lorries.

Loose wheat was formerly carted back to the farm to be built into stacks. Mechanised balers eliminated the need for stacks but required larger fields so hedgerows were grubbed up.

St Bartholomew, Chipping

St Andrew, Congham

Lancaster Priory

St Clare, Bradfield St Clare

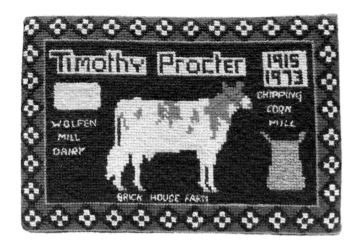

Brick House Farm diversified, adding cheese-making and milling to its activities. *St Bartholomew, Chipping*

An orphaned lamb, or one thought to be dangerously frail, would be brought into the kitchen for warmth and bottle-feeding. The kitchen was also useful for drying boots. *St Andrew, Congham*

Sheep did not lend themselves to industrial farming, unlike unfortunate pigs. *St Bartholomew, Chipping*

St Mary, Steeple Barton

WORK

In peacetime Britain, the world of work was changing. The old master/servant attitude had no place in modern industry. Employer/employee relationships placed rights and responsibilities on both sides.

The Waterman's Company. Today's members of this livery company are probably less obsequious and less good at rowing. *Chelsea Old Church, London*

Seat cushions in Lancaster Priory record some of the city's trades unions.

The National Union of Students, National Farmers' Union and the British Medical Association are represented here.

The Amalgamated Union of Building Trade Workers, National Union of Teachers and the Embroiderers' Guild.

The National Union of Railwaymen and the Associated Society of Locomotive Engineers and Firemen – oddly linked with Hornsea Pottery.

Workers by Hand and by Brain

Berry & Sons' chairs had a
high reputation for comfort.
St Bartholomew, Chipping

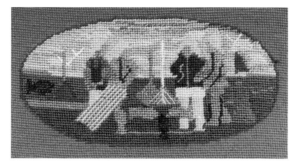

Fishermen prepare their nets.
St Michael, Framlingham

A farrier gets down to the job.
All Saints, Brandeston

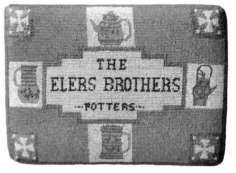

John and David Elers were Dutch
silversmiths who came to England in the
1680s, becoming innovative potters,
noted for their redware.
Chelsea Old Church, London

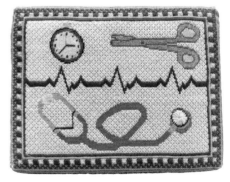

A doctor uses old and new technology.
St Andrew, Much Hadham

This cushion is a recognition of the complexity of work involved in administering Lancaster Borough Council. The work of designing and stitching such an intricate tribute to local government should also be recognised.

The lion and fleur de lys refer to the borough's coat of arms. The emblems – not all easy to identify – represent municipal services. A house and a tree refer to the Borough's Housing and Parks. Education is marked by lollipop men on zebra crossings. Two steam rollers illustrate road maintenance. Taps represent the water supply while the public baths are shown twice over. A cross perhaps represents the borough's cemeteries. Libraries, law courts, hospitals, concert halls and the art gallery are identifiable. Town Planning, Weights and Measures and Refuse Disposal are also illustrated, according to the Lancaster Priory's guide to its canvaswork, but which emblem represents Town Planning? Which represents Refuse Disposal? And the police are apparently illustrated, but where? *Lancaster Priory*

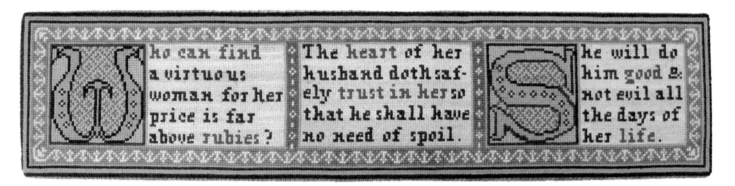

Multitasking by women has been the experience of centuries.

The duties of women are translated into the activities to be found in a Norfolk village. Whatever your views on King Solomon, this is a glorious series.

In St Andrew, Congham, Norfolk, the kneeler sequence is inspired by the Book of Proverbs in which King Solomon spells out the attributes of a Virtuous Woman: the views of the Queen of Sheba are not known.

She riseth also while it is yet night.

She worketh willingly with her hands.

She looketh well to the ways of her household, and eateth not the bread of idleness. (Prov. 31: 15, 17 and 27)

THE PLEASURES OF PEACETIME

When not at work, people were able to indulge themselves in a multiplicity of activities.

The public joined the National Trust in millions to protect open spaces and historic sites.
St John the Baptist, Danbury

Women's Institutes were founded in Canada to encourage the revitalisation of rural areas. The first branch in the UK was launched in 1915 at Llanfairpwll in Anglesey. The WI focused at first on producing food, and in the Second World War it was also involved in the care of evacuees. During peacetime, its ambitions for women widened still further.
St Mary the Virgin, Friston

The pleasures of peacetime included much stitching. Hooray for Olive Procter and all designers and makers of kneelers that are local, original and unique!
St Bartholomew, Chipping

Much pleasure comes from hard work, concentration and practice.

Sewing
St Andrew, Congham

Gardening
St Michael and All Angels, Onibury

Music
St Andrew, Much Hadham

Cycling
St Mary's, Barnes

Fishing
St Mary, Stratford St Mary

Bee-keeping
St Peter, Tewin

All Work and No Play . . .

Sport means different things to different people. I hate competitive games and always fell off the pony when I tried to jump. Others are not like me.

... the run-stealers flicker to and fro,
To and fro: O my Hornby and my Barlow long ago!

'At Lords', Francis Thompson

St Michael and All Angels, Ledbury

'Football is not about life and death, it is more important than that.' Bill Shankly, manager of Liverpool FC, was apparently slightly misquoted, but the aphorism is widely enjoyed.
St Michael and All Angels, Howick

My games mistress, despairing, once warned me: 'If you don't play tennis, you'll never get married!' Fortunately, I met someone who didn't play tennis. *St Peter, Tewin*

Oh, wasn't it naughty of Smudges?
Oh, Mummy, I'm sick with disgust.
She threw me in front of the judges
And my silly old collarbone's bust.

'Hunter Trials', John Betjeman

St Andrew, Much Hadham

TRANSPORT AND TRAVEL

Railways opened up the country in the nineteenth century. In the twentieth, the internal combustion engine allowed people to travel by cars and buses. The jet engine enabled distant air travel.

Steam engines were on the way out, but stitchers remained nostalgic. Diesel and electric trains have failed to capture their fancy. *St Mary Magdalene, Woodstock*

A steam train thunders over a viaduct. *St Peter, Tewin*

Buses helped to open up the countryside to schoolchildren and shoppers. *St Peter, Tewin*

This vehicle would have astonished John Tower's parents in 1888. By 1954, it was a collector's item.
St Bartholomew, Chipping

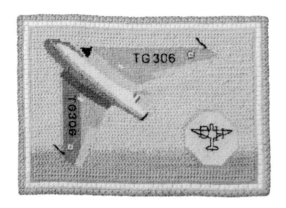

The de Havilland DH 108 Swallow was an experimental tailless jet which proved unstable. It crashed, 27 September 1946, killing its pilot, Geoffrey de Havilland. But 1940s engineering ingenuity and the dedication of test pilots led to today's reliable air transport. *St Peter, Tewin*

Square-wheeled lorries thunder along the A14. But what is the blue shape on the verge? Litter? Or a crashed car? Has the individual – bottom right – just escaped? Is this kneeler a votive offering? *All Saints, Sproughton*

A Concorde passes over St Mary's Church in Barnes – a sight no longer seen. At least double-decker red buses continue to drive past the church.

ANGELS AND ARCHANGELS

After Lucifer, son of the morning, fell from heaven, angels had no more fighting to do and became messengers of God.

Some angels are angels of power. *St Andrew, Much Hadham*

The Archangel St Michael and his angels cast out *that old serpent, called the Devil* onto the earth. (Rev. 12: 9) He landed in North Radnorshire and St Michael scooped a great hill on top of him, planted it with Radnor Forest and pinned it down with five churches dedicated to himself and his angels. (Monoglot English need to know that the three churches called Llanfihangel are dedicated to St Michael.) *St Michael and All Angels, Ledbury*

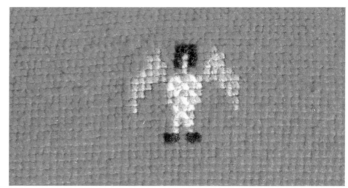

Some angels are not. The stitcher feared that this small angel might spend eternity standing on a cloud. Galoshes are a practical introduction that will help to keep the angelic feet dry and therefore warmer. *Holy Trinity, Hardwicke*

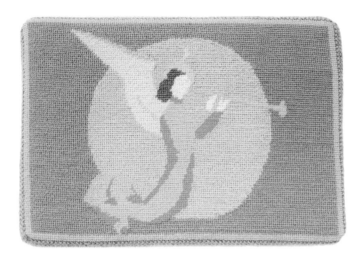

While shepherds watched their flock by night: *And, lo, the angel of the Lord came upon them . . . and said: 'Fear not: for, behold, I bring you good tidings of great joy . . .'*
St Mary's, Raydon

The sheep were abandoned as their shepherds hurried to Bethlehem to see the infant Christ. Two angels were assigned to guard duty to protect the flock from wolves.
St Mary Magdalene, Woodstock

And suddenly there was with the angel a multitude of the heavenly host praising God, and saying, 'Glory to God in the highest, and on earth peace, good will toward men' (St Luke 2: 9–14).
St Michael and All Angels, Ledbury

SUPERNATURAL LIFE

Beyond the everyday is the eternal struggle between good and evil.

Lazily, illustrators have chosen to ignore St John of Patmos' carefully described physical attributes of the great Satan and to rely on the easily available pictures of dragons. Stitchers of course knew the difference between dragons and the Devil.

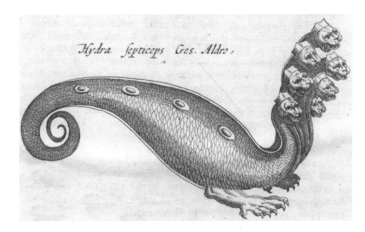

St John of Patmos describes the Devil: 'Behold a great red dragon, having seven heads and ten horns, and seven crowns upon his heads'. He also calls him: 'That old serpent called the Devil'. Is he a dragon or is he a serpent? These medieval illustrators settled on a 'hydra'.

Examine the images of red dragons. None of these has seven heads or ten horns, therefore none represents the Devil.

St Andrew, Much Hadham

St Mary Magdalene, Woodstock

St Edmund, Southwold

Brainwashed by St George, the English equated dragons –
even green ones! – with Hitler. And here Hitler is getting
his comeuppance. *St Margaret, St Margaret's, Herefordshire*

This unfortunate herbivore had been peacefully grazing on wild
leeks. Suddenly he finds himself threatened by a young tough
with a bladed weapon. He tries to calm the situation but it's
bound to end badly. *St Andrew, Much Hadham*

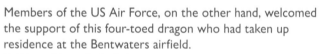

Members of the US Air Force, on the other hand, welcomed the support of this four-toed dragon who had taken up residence at the Bentwaters airfield.
St Edmundsbury Cathedral

Dragons can be benevolent, as the Welsh have always known. In Raydon, Suffolk, this dragon is the parish watchdog, ready to shrivel invaders from the east with its flaming breath. Its guardianship has been entirely successful and neither Napoleon nor Hitler ever succeeded in capturing Raydon.
St Mary's, Raydon

In nearby All Saints, Laxfield, the friendly, flower-breathing dragon has neither legs nor wings.

He has been joined by a couple of Tritons – one young, one old. These are sea gods who can raise a storm or calm a sea with a blast on a conch horn but have little interest in humans. Or dragons. Or any land-based life form.

Gorgons are different. According to Patrick Leigh Fermor in *Mani*, mermaids with double tails are 'gorgona'.[10] He asserts that they are descendants of Medusa, mutations over the centuries having led to the shrivelling of snakes back into hairs and the shrivelling of legs into fish tails. They are known for luring young shepherds and young sailors to their deaths, but this is not all. Leigh Fermor cites the thirteenth-century Byzantine bestiary, *O Physiologos*, which describes gorgons as being 'tormented by wantonness and lusting after lions and dragons and other beasts'. But this double-tailed, three-headed gorgon shows no sign of being tormented by wantonness.

All Saints, Laxfield

Some of the matings that took place in Laxfield between the gorgona and the local dragon led to mutations that turned the second head into that of a blonde woman. The first of their progeny seem happy enough, but the second seems less contented, while the third – with a Picasso-like double eye and cubist nose – seems sunk in gloom.

All Saints, Laxfield

HIGHLIGHTS, QUIRKS AND ODDITIES

In Quenington, Gloucestershire, the kneeler designer Enid Money, like other folk artists, was not interested in pictorial realism. She preferred to tell a story.

St Francis is preaching – inside or maybe outside a church – to the birds and beasts of God's creation. The crocodile is gobsmacked. The owl listens attentively. The stork has only just arrived. A bat flutters in. None of them sees the helpful angel delivering St Francis' halo. *St Swithin, Quenington*

It takes two angels to honour St Joseph – one with a trumpet and one with his halo. St Joseph fails to notice because his dog wants to go for a walk. *St Swithin, Quenington*

In Bradfield St Clare, Suffolk, retired headmaster George Insley, looking out of his spare bedroom window, began sketching the view on the back of an old piece of wallpaper. He had had no previous experience of design or of stitching but the altar-rail kneelers and seat cushions that he then produced in the late 1970s are among the most beautiful I have come across.

I suspect that Mr Insley transferred his sketch from his bit of wallpaper to graph paper simply to establish correct proportions and relationships. Then there must have been a lengthy process of stitching, unpicking and re-stitching to achieve the realism of the furrows and the delicacy of the clouds.

St Clare, Bradfield St Clare

Celebrating Church Features

Stitchers always liked to focus on the local and could hardly get more local than recording features from their own church.

This records a graffito on the wall of All Saints' south transept about Simon and Nellie, a quarrelsome couple made particularly unreasonable by poverty. They were reduced to their final lump of dough. 'Boil it,' said Simon. 'Bake it,' demanded Nellie. She clouted him. He whacked her back. Finally they agreed to boil it first and then to bake it. They had invented Simnel cake.
All Saints, Leighton Buzzard

An elephant's head rising out of a bed of lilies, here reproduced in cross stitch, is one of the church's many brightly coloured roof bosses.
St Mary, Ottery St Mary

The stitchers of this altar rail kneeler are proud of their church's sixteenth-century poor box.

All Saints, Dovercourt

The Laxfield stitcher sets the clock at Grantchester time. It would have encouraged Rupert Brooke.

Stands the church clock at ten to three?
And is there honey still for tea?

'The Old Vicarage, Grantchester', Rupert Brooke

All Saints, Laxfield

Unusual Texts

Not all texts come in English and even the English ones ignore standardised spellings.

This kneeler repeats the prayer – in which we can all join without reservation – inscribed on the almshouses in Leighton Buzzard. *All Saints, Leighton Buzzard*

The Sator Square is thought to have been a way in which the early Christians, at a time of persecution, could secretly announce their presence to each other. The square itself is a series of palindromes, while the words *SATOR AREPO TENET OPERA ROTAS* can also be translated as 'The sower holds the works and wheels by means of water'. Perhaps the words made better sense to early Christians. The square can also be used to spell out 'Paternoster', the Latin name for the Lord's Prayer, with the residual letters (two As and two Os) symbolising Alpha and Omega. *St Nicholas, Charlwood*

Here Joshua declares in Hebrew: *As for me and my house, we will serve the Lord* (Josh. 24: 15). *St Peter, Langford Budville*

The Musings of the Master

Noël Coward said that he merely had 'a talent to amuse'.
His fans have always known him as the Master.

Mad dogs and Englishmen go out in the midday sun.
St Peter, Tewin

The stately homes of England
How beautiful they stand
To show the upper classes
Have still the upper hand.
St Andrew, Congham

Don't put your daughter on the stage, Mrs Worthington,
Don't put your daughter on the stage [. . .]
On my knees, Mrs Worthington,
Please, Mrs Worthington,
Don't put your daughter on the stage.
St Peter, Tewin

Three Parishes with a Single Design

Anglican kneeler-makers clearly like visiting Ravenna to study the mosaics in the fifth-century Roman Mausoleum of Galla Placidia. The bird bath seems to be their favourite.

Holy Trinity, Bradford-on-Avon

St Mary Magdalene, Woodstock

St Andrew, Much Hadham

Odd

In the twenty-first chapter of the Book of Revelation, there is a description of *that great city, the holy Jerusalem, descending out of heaven from God*. It had no houses in it, just a great, high wall with twelve gates – three on each of its four sides. *And the wall of the city had twelve foundations [. . .] And the foundations of the city were garnished with all manner of precious stones.* (Rev. 21: 10–19)

Odder

The National Gallery has this depiction, by the Renaissance artist Sassetta, of the Holy Jerusalem. It hovers above the sleeping St Francis who is dreaming of it. Note that Sassetta shows the city only. Its twelve foundations have been left behind.

Oddest

Here the stitcher in St Andrew, Much Hadham is acting as a celestial archaeologist, patiently recording the different ornamented layers of the holy city's foundations. In the long histories of art and of folk art, I don't believe these have been recorded before.

The first foundation's garnish – jasper – is shown at the bottom left. Some of the stones – sapphire, emerald, topaz and amethyst – are easy to recognise, the others less so.

On the bottom layer, starting from the left, the third, fifth and sixth are chalcedony, sardonyx and sardius. On the upper register the seventh, eighth, tenth and eleventh are chrysolite, beryl, chrysoprasus and jacinth.

Practical Information

TECHNIQUES FOR TRANSFERRING DESIGNS ONTO CANVAS

For several decades after the war, designs for kneelers were drawn in pencil on graph paper. This required stitchers to count stitches to match the design.

This is a partial and inaccurate representation of what the design for the Three Kings kneeler at St Mary, Stratford St Mary would have looked like. I've left out the stars blazing away in the midday sun – they've clearly been powered up by the brilliant star that guides the Kings. I've also left out – through laziness – the outline of the pyramidical hills.

The point of this drawing is to show the care the designer has taken to make counting easy for the stitcher. The camel's tail is two stitches away from the second King. The third King is not only close but has the first palm tree conveniently growing out of his arm.

Today, though, people maintain that they cannot count. And A3 graph paper, ten squares to the inch to match the squares on the kneeler canvas, is no longer freely available. Technology has also helped to bring about the demise of much authentic folk art.

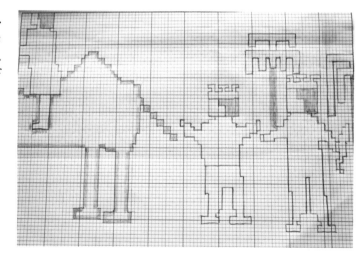

The arrival of print shops meant that it was easy to crop or enlarge pictures or photographs to fit the kneeler design. The outline of the central feature could then be traced onto graph paper, giving nervous designers confidence, after which they could add extra embellishments. In the case of the goosander shown here, they could add ripples or reeds or reflections.

The many different angles of roof and wall surfaces of this forge, sheds and house in St Barnabas, Brampton Bryan, Herefordshire, would have been simple to copy from a photograph blown up to kneeler size.

But I wrote this before meeting the stitcher who told me she had worked out and stitched the design directly onto the canvas. I was right: tracing a photograph would have been simpler – but she was more skilled than me.

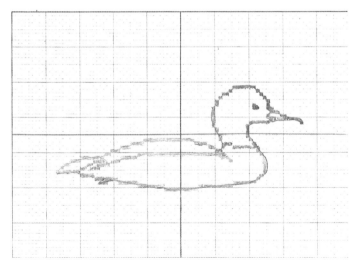

TECHNOLOGY-ASSISTED COMMUNITY ART

Some communities like to copy the work of favourite artists. There is a long tradition of artists – Raphael, Goya, John Piper – creating designs for tapestries, and the advent of modern lightboxes has just varied and updated the tradition. A patient stitcher can transfer any suitable picture with paints to kneeler canvas. All that then has to be done is match the wools to the painted colour.

In Howick, Northumberland, the community wanted to create new canvaswork kneelers for their church, St Michael and All Angels. The congregation wanted images of local scenes or events and recruited local artists to submit designs. They successfully applied for a grant and the work of selecting designs was launched.

Here, parishioner Melita Butterell is using her skill and a lightbox to transfer the work of a local artist to a kneeler canvas. Her assiduity makes it possible for a stitcher to follow a far more detailed type of design than outlines on graph paper can easily display.

This swallow kneeler shows one of Howick's lightbox-enabled designs with details that would have been hard to reproduce on graph paper at ten squares to the inch.

STITCHING

Most folk-art kneelers are in simple cross stitch – hard-wearing and easy to do. Anyone who has played noughts and crosses knows that the cross is one diagonal over another. No training or experience is required.

The skilled, and also the adventurous, are in the minority. They explore the many variations of cross stitch that exist, giving a textural dimension. In St Mary the Virgin, Stanwell, Surrey, stitchers used Lisbeth Perrone's book *The New World of Needlepoint* which describes '101 exciting designs in Bargello, Quickpoint, Grospoint and other repeat patterns'. Stitchers chose a favourite stitch for the side of their kneelers, making the sides quick to finish and marking their contribution.

When I began kneeler-making, I was so uninformed that when an expert suggested that I should do the background in Basketweave Tent, I was baffled. The names of different stitches led to panic – I knew I would never master Irregular Byzantine or Gobelin Encroaching, let alone Oblong Double-Tied Cross. I remained regrettably unadventurous and have only ever used cross stitch for my designs.

St Paul's shipwreck is stitched by Ailsie Corble in petit point at twenty tent stitches to the inch, with the frame and background in straightforward gros point at ten cross stitches to the inch. *St Mary Abbots, Kensington*

This memorial kneeler to thatcher Harry Jones shows the metal of the shears and of the wire-brush bristles in petit point and the wooden thatching tool in a variety of cross stitches. The three tools are set against a strongly textured background.
St Michael and All Angels, Onibury

The mice are in cross stitch, with stitches crossed to the left on the left-hand mouse and to the right on the right-hand mouse. Their claws are in French stitch. The shelf is in upright gobelin; the green book pages in long-armed cross stitch; and the candles in flat stitch with the plumes of melted wax in French knots.
St Mary Magdalene, Woodstock

In Winchester Cathedral, designs by the great Guy Barton make little impact at the head of the nave. Anna Diamond of the Cathedral Broderers decided, therefore, on simple patterns in blue – the colour of the heavens, of the Virgin's robe and of the Evensong booklets – with complex and intriguing textures. It may be heretical to hope that some stitches are Irregular Byzantine.

Winchester Cathedral

This otter is shown with long stitches following the curve of its body and marking its bristling whiskers. Its mask is in small cross stitches. A variety of stitches pick out plants against the different background stitches. The long stitches may not prove hard-wearing but as the practice of kneeling is in decline one hopes the long stitches may survive along with the local otters.

St Michael and All Angels, Howick

EPILOGUE

The movement to beautify churches with kneelers of original designs coincided closely with the reign of Queen Elizabeth II. After the long years of war and post-war austerity, the accession of the young Queen coincided with emerging prosperity. Stitchers once again could engage in decorative needlework. Parishes across the country began to celebrate their local environment – built and natural – and to create memorials to past events, to local bigwigs and to their own parishioners. And people – male and female – were then accustomed to stitching and to following patterns. All who could follow the complexities of a knitting pattern found following graph paper designs a doddle.

In the early fifties, horses were still drawing ploughs. By the time of Queen Elizabeth's death, jets flashed across the skies and nuclear power stations pumped out clean energy.

Folk art kneelers over the time of her reign were an illustration of social change. But social change also affected the churches. Pews were ripped out. Congregations became reluctant to kneel. Kneelers were felt to be redundant and were stored away or disposed of.

The millennium saw a brief moment of revival. One of the finest kneeler projects in the country can be found in St Peter, Tewin, in Hertfordshire. But as time passed, designers and stitchers became fewer. And now Anglican folk art has all but fizzled out.

I hope this book may at least encourage congregations with interesting locally-designed kneelers to preserve them. They form a small but delightful footnote to the history of art during the reign of the late monarch and are worth treasuring.

If you've enjoyed a gentle look at all the kneelers in this book,
Why not return it to the shelf and go and see them for yourself?

'Envoi', Sam Norman

Jasper. *St Peter, Langford Budville*

ACKNOWLEDGEMENTS

My gratitude, first and foremost, is to the designers of the kneelers and cushions that are the subject of this book, and, secondly, to the parishes that embraced and stitched their designs. Clergy and parishioners, including the helpful members of the Tewin, Langford Budville, Leighton Buzzard, Congham, Raydon, Laxfield and Howick congregations, among others, have been immensely generous in supplying me with photographs and information.

This book grew out of the website, parishkneelers. co.uk, that I began many decades ago. It developed from a meeting with Laurence and Ruth Clarke of Southwold. Their comprehensive survey of the original kneelers to be found in East Suffolk made me aware of the diversity and vitality of this new form of folk art.

People at Chatto & Windus were immensely supportive. Rose Davidson, with a formidable mastery of the internet, introduced me to valuable sources of information – such as Eusebius – which I would never have discovered on my own. And I had an instant meeting of minds with Amanda Waters, who shared my delight in this small niche in the art history of twentieth-century Britain. She persuaded me of the necessity of replacing amateur iPhone pictures with high-quality photographs. This – in combination with Will Webb's masterly layout – has strikingly improved the book.

I was lucky in the professional photographers who supplied me. S. J. Newman not only supplied the glorious pictures of Sybil Blunt's cushions but also told me of the collection of her watercolours owned by the Friends of Winchester Cathedral: they were a revelation. Martyn Mackie's photographs made readable the complexity of Guy Barton's designs: check out the Lancaster Borough Council cushion on page 108. Victoria Harrison patiently returned to local churches to expand and upgrade the record. Billie Charity photographed tussocks, kneelers and me with aplomb. And Seb Morton found new kneelers that had been added to collections that I had researched a decade or two ago.

And how could an octogenarian novice produce a book without family support? My son, Harry, of jerichowriters.com, doubled the length of my first draft by demanding an historical introduction. My granddaughter, Rose, painted a flattering portrait of her aunt Kate. My grandson, Sam, provided the book's closing lines. And, finally, this book would never have been written without endless bullying from my kid cousin, Caroline Dawnay. Reader, I gave in. She's now my agent.

NOTES

1 The Imperial War Museum (www.iwm.org.uk/collections/item/object/30083764).

2 *Spring Cannot Be Cancelled* by David Hockney and Martin Gayford (Thames and Hudson Ltd, 2021).

3 *From the Holy Mountain* by William Dalrymple (HarperCollins, 1997).

4 'hassock, n.' (*OED online*, Oxford University Press, www.oed.com).

5 John Barlow FRS (1799–1869).

6 Information on the Norfolk cushions and those from Pembroke College, Cambridge, and Brasenose College, Oxford, is drawn from '"The Beauty of Holiness": Armorial Turkey-work cushions for use in religious settings in the Commonwealth and Restoration' by Sarah Medlam and Annabel Westman (*Furniture History*, Vol. LIII, pp. 13–26).

7 Information on Berlin work is drawn from *Victorian Canvas Work* by Molly G. Proctor (Batsford Embroidery Paperbacks, Batsford Ltd, 1986).

8 'Lancaster Privateer Beat Napoleon's Ship', (*Lancs Live*, 13 June 2021, www.lancs.live/news/lancashire-news/lancaster-privateer-beat-napole-ons-ship-20769660).

9 'Thetis (1801 ship)', (*Wikipedia, The Free Encyclopedia*, 5 December 2022, en.wikipedia.org/w/index.php?title=Thetis_(1801_ship)&oldid=1125796939).

10 *Mani* by Patrick Leigh Fermor (John Murray, 1958).

ILLUSTRATION CREDITS

The authors and publishers are grateful to the following for permission to reproduce photographs from:

All Hallows by the Tower, City of London © Amanda Waters
All Saints, Brandeston © Will Webb
All Saints, Brandeston, p.74 © Victoria Harrison Photography
All Saints, Laxfield © Will Webb
All Saints, Leighton Buzzard © The Reverend Cate Irvine
All Saints, Sproughton © Ralph Earey
Bradfield St Clare © Victoria Harrison Photography
Chalfont St Giles © Helen Rayner Photography
Chelsea Old Church © Connie Swift
Derby Cathedral © John Kemp
Hereford Cathedral © Billie Charity Photography
Lancaster Priory Church of St Mary © Martyn Mackie Photography
St Andrew, Congham © Mark Scase
St Andrew, Much Hadham © David Calvert Photography
St Andrew, Wissett © Victoria Harrison Photography
St Bartholomew, Chipping © Martyn Mackie Photography
St Clement Danes, City of London © Amanda Waters
St Cynog, Boughrood © Billie Charity Photography
St Cyriac, Lacock © Lacock Photography
St David, Llanfaes © Billie Charity Photography
St Denys, Evington © Louise Kelham Photography
St Edmund, Southwold © Victoria Harrison Photography
St John the Baptist, Danbury © Hammonds Photography Studio
St Mary's, Barnes © Amanda Waters
St Mary's, Raydon © Victoria Harrison Photography
St Mary's, Raydon, p. 120 © Simon Tennent
St Mary, Steeple Barton © Ian Taylor Photography
St Mary Abbots, Kensington © Amanda Waters
St Mary Magdalene, Woodstock © Sebastian Morton
St Michael, Framlingham © Will Webb

St Michael, Highgate © Amanda Waters
St Michael and All Angels, Howick © Stewart Sexton
St Michael and All Angels, Ledbury © Billie Charity Photography
St Michael and All Angels, Ledbury, p. 112 © Paul Ligas Photography
St Nicholas, Charlwood © The Reverend Sue Wheakley
St Peter, Langford Budville © Saranne Cessford
St Peter, Tewin © Rose Davidson
St Swithin, Quenington © Kay Ransom Photography
Stratford St Mary © Victoria Harrison Photography
Wadham College Chapel kneelers: photographs by Julia Banfield © The Warden and Fellows of Wadham College. Reproduced by kind permission of the Warden and Fellows of Wadham College
Winchester Cathedral: Sibyl Blunt cushions and kneelers. Photography by S. J. Newman © The Dean & Chapter of Winchester 2019. Reproduced by kind permission of The Dean & Chapter of Winchester
Winchester Cathedral nave kneeler, p. 49, by Anna Diamond

p. 14: hassock and tussock © Billie Charity Photography; p. 16: Aunt Kate © Rose Bingham; p. 28: Wadham College Chapel entrance arch © Amanda Waters; pp. 40, 42, 44, 45, 46, 47: Sibyl Blunt sketches. Photograph S. J. Newman © Friends of Winchester Cathedral; p. 49: Illustration from *Historical Designs for Embroidery* by Louisa Pesel, B. T. Batsford, 1956 © public domain; p. 53: Chelsea Old Church Bomb Damage © Topical Press Agency/Hulton Archive/Gettyimages; p. 118: Picture of Hydra from *Historiae naturalis de serpentibus libri II*, by Joannes Jonstonus, 1665; p. 131: *Saint Francis and the Poor Knight, and Francis's Vision* by Sassetta © The National Gallery, London; p. 135: Goosander from *A History of British Birds* by The Reverend F. O. Morris. Illustrated by Alexander Francis Lydon and printed by B. Fawcett, 1863–1867; p. 136: Photograph of Melita Butterell at St Michael and All Angels, Howick © David Butterell

Every effort has been made to trace and contact all holders of copyright in illustrations. If there are any inadvertent omissions or errors, the publishers will be pleased to correct these at the earliest opportunity.